Why do fish bite?

Copyright © Miles Kelly Publishing Ltd 2008

This edition published 2009

2 4 6 8 10 9 7 5 3 1

Editorial Director Belinda Gallagher
Art Director Jo Brewer
Editorial Assistant Carly Blake
Volume Designer Sally Lace
Cover Designer Jo Brewer
Indexer Hilary Bird
Production Manager Elizabeth Brunwin
Reprographics Anthony Cambray, Ian Paulyn
Editions Manager Bethan Ellish
Character Cartoonist Mike Foster

All artwork from the Miles Kelly Archives

ISBN 978-1-84810-120-3

Printed in China

British Library Cataloguing-in-Publication Data
A catalogue record for this book is available
from the British Library

Made with paper from a sustainable forest

www.mileskelly.net
info@mileskelly.net

www.factsforprojects.com
The one-stop homework helper —
pictures, facts, videos, projects and more

Contents

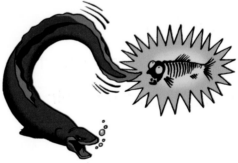

Why do hippos attack each other?

Male hippos attack each other to defend the patch of land where they live. When they fight, hippos stand face-to-face with their mouths wide-open, and slash and swipe at each other with their tusk-like teeth. Sometimes these fights end in the death of one, or both of the hippos.

Hippos

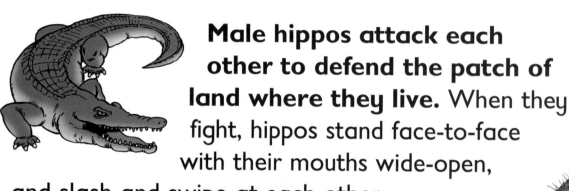

Explore
Ants live in most places, even in your garden. Take a look outside and see if you can spot any.

Which bird can kill while it flies?

The peregrine falcon can, and this is called hunting 'on the wing'. It's the fastest hunting animal in the world and flies at 230 kilometres an hour. Peregrine falcons chase their prey before attacking it to tire it out.

Hold it, hippopotamus!

Hippos and whales are closely related – maybe this is why they can hold their breath under water for 12 minutes!

Do army ants go hunting?

Army ants hunt in groups, sometimes of more than one million ants. They move forward in a wave across the ground. Ants at the front of the group kill insects and small lizards in their path, while ants further back carry food to the nest.

Army
ants

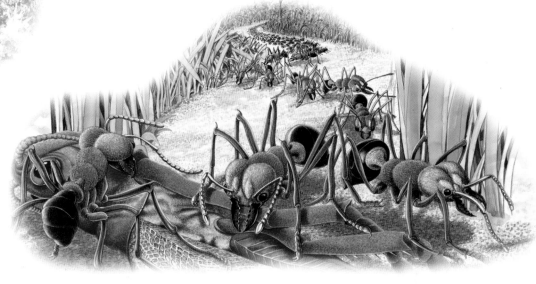

Why do snakes have fangs?

Poisonous snakes such as rattlesnakes have an extra-long pair of teeth called fangs. A deadly poison called venom runs along a groove in each fang. When the snake bites an animal, its fangs sink into the animal's skin and venom is injected.

Rattlesnake →

Discover

Some eels use electricity to hunt. What things in your home use electricity?

Which creature kills with its tail?

All scorpions have a poisonous sting in their tail. They use their front claw-like arms to hold their prey, while their tail-sting injects a harmful venom. Few scorpions can badly injure a human, but a sting from the death stalker scorpion can cause death.

Death stalker scorpion

Death match!

Scorpions normally live alone because most of them eat other scorpions. If two scorpions meet, they will fight to the death and the loser is eaten by the winner.

Why are eels shocking?

Electric eels use electricity to zap their prey and to attack other animals that they are threatened by. The electric eel, which is actually a type of fish, can produce up to 600 volts of electricty – enough to kill a human!

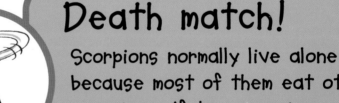

Which deadly fish looks like a stone?

The stonefish looks just like a piece of coral-covered rock or stone on the seabed. It sits and waits for its prey to come close. Then the stonefish strikes out at lightning speed and gobbles up its victim. For defence, the stonefish is covered in poisonous spikes.

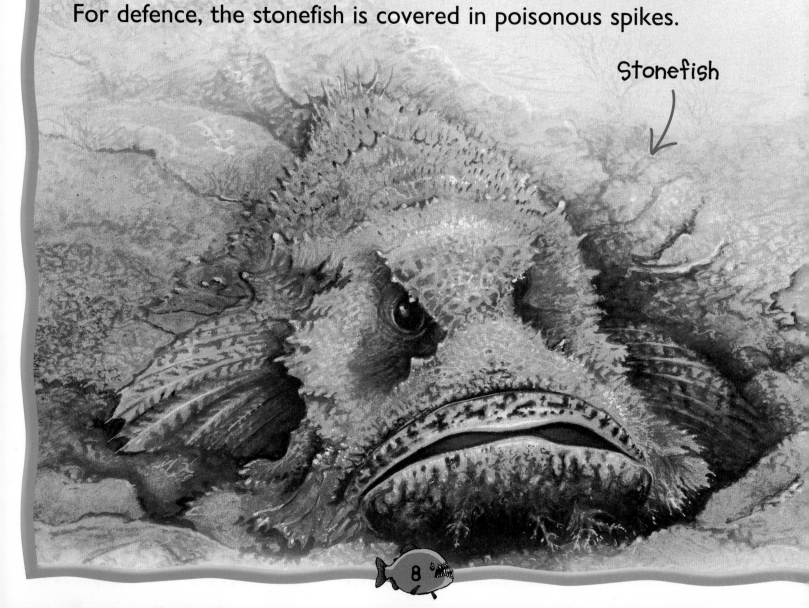

Stonefish

What do animals use their tusks for?

Tusks are overgrown teeth, and animals such as walruses and elephants use their tusks as weapons to stab and swipe at attackers. Males use them to fight one another during the mating season.

Hornet

Can insects be deadly?

Many insects, even small ones, can harm other animals. Bees, wasps and hornets have stings in their tails that can inject venom. A sting from one of these insects can cause swelling and pain, and even death to some people.

King sting!

The world's largest hornet is the Asian giant hornet. Its body is up to 4.5 centimetres long and its stinger is 6 millimetres long.

Why do crocodiles have big teeth?

Crocodiles have lots of big teeth for catching their prey. A crocodile's diet includes fish, birds and mammals, such as gazelle and wildebeest. The crocodile's sharp teeth and powerful jaws help it to keep hold of its prey and to bite chunks off to swallow.

Nile crocodile

Do snakes eat people?

Pythons, such as Burmese pythons, have been known to attack and kill humans, but this is very rare. Small mammals and birds are normal foods for a python, which can open its mouth wide enough to swallow big animals such as pigs and deer whole!

Make

Using an old sock for the body, buttons for eyes and wooden pegs for teeth, make a crocodile glove puppet.

Boiled eggs!

Whether a baby crocodile is a female or a male depends on temperature. A female will develop in a warm egg and a male will develop in a cool egg.

What is a deathspin?

A deathspin is what crocodiles and alligators do to drown their prey. A crocodile pulls its victim underwater and twists and turns until the animal is dead. The crocodiles's strong jaws keep a grip on the animal as it rolls and turns in the water.

What is a black widow?

The black widow is one of the world's most deadly spiders. Black widows only bite if they are disturbed. Male black widows are harmless, but a bite from a female can kill a human. Sometimes, the female black widow eats the male after mating.

Black widow

Think

Lots of people are scared of spiders. Are there any creepy-crawlies that you are afraid of?

Why do fish bite?

Piranhas are small fish with razor-sharp teeth. They can be very fierce and will bite anything that they think they can eat. Piranhas usually hunt alone but may gather in groups to attack larger animals, which they strip to the bone in minutes.

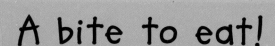

A bite to eat!

Piranhas are found in rivers in South America and are often caught for food by the local people. Their teeth are used in weapons and tools.

Piranhas

Why do crocodiles eat rotting meat?

Crocodiles eat rotting meat because it is easier to swallow. Crocodiles and alligators store their food by wedging the dead animal under an underwater branch or log, so that it rots down. Sometimes, they store their food for several weeks.

Which bat eats bones?

False vampire bats kill their prey by biting its head or neck and crushing its skull. Then it swallows the flesh, bones, teeth, fur and even feathers of its prey. Its favourite foods are birds, as well as lizards, frogs and mice.

False vampire bat →

Flies for tea!

Most bats eat insects. They catch their prey by snatching it out of the air while flying. Some bats will catch around 2000 insects in one night!

When is jelly dangerous?

When it's an Australian box jellyfish — the deadliest jellyfish in the world. The body of the box jellyfish is harmless, but one touch from its tentacles can kill a human. Box jellyfish are also known as 'sea wasps'.

Wear

Try on some colourful, bright clothes, like the poison-dart frog. How many colours are in your outfit?

Why are some frogs brightly coloured?

The green poison-dart frog is brightly coloured to tell attackers to stay away. These frogs also make a poisonous slime on their skin. Local people of South America wipe the poison onto the ends of their hunting darts because it's strong enough to kill animals such as monkeys.

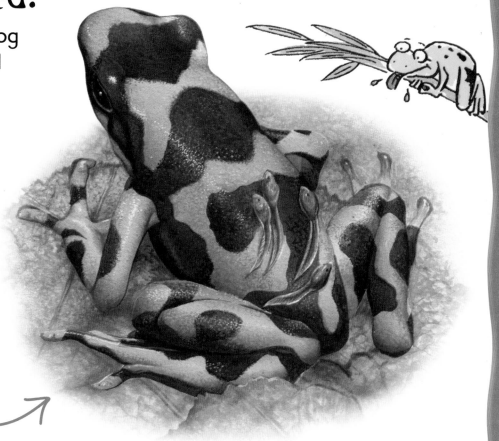

Poison-dart frog

15

What is the deadliest lizard?

The Komodo dragon is the deadliest, and biggest, meat-eating lizard. It eats every part of an animal, including bones. The germs in a Komodo dragon's mouth can cause a deadly infection to an animal that escapes with just a bite.

Komodo dragon

How do coyotes catch their prey?

Coyotes are fast runners and often chase speedy jackrabbits across rocks and up hills. When hunting larger animals such as deer, a group of coyotes chase the animal to tire it out and bite its neck to stop it breathing.

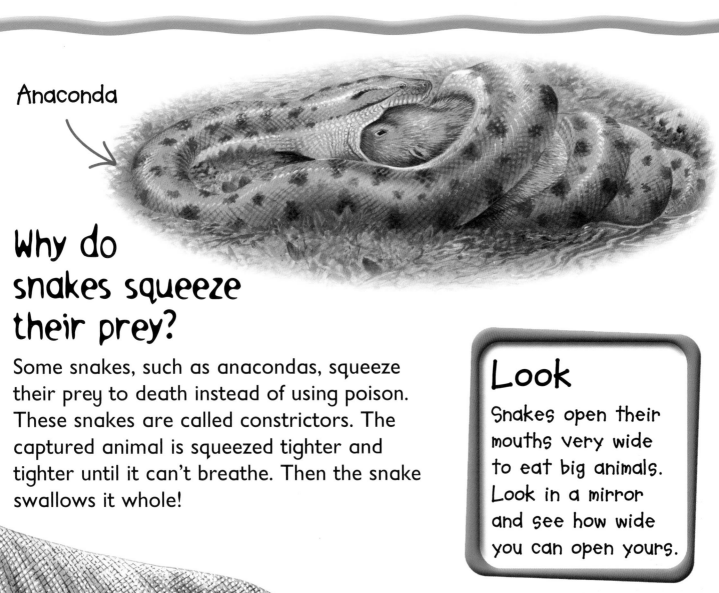

Anaconda

Why do snakes squeeze their prey?

Some snakes, such as anacondas, squeeze their prey to death instead of using poison. These snakes are called constrictors. The captured animal is squeezed tighter and tighter until it can't breathe. Then the snake swallows it whole!

Look

Snakes open their mouths very wide to eat big animals. Look in a mirror and see how wide you can open yours.

Deadly down under!

Australia has more poisonous snakes for its size than any other country — including eight of the world's ten deadliest snakes.

Can monkeys be dangerous?

Mandrills are the biggest type of monkey, and they can be dangerous. Their fangs grow up to 7 centimetres long and are used as deadly weapons to attack weaker mandrills in their group. Males also show their teeth to impress females during the mating season.

Mandrill

Draw

Using colouring pencils, draw a picture of a monkey. See if you can make it as colourful as this mandrill.

Why do wolves snarl?

Wolves snarl when they are angry or threatened by another animal. When a wolf snarls, its lips curls back to show its long, sharp teeth and its nostrils widen. The fur on the wolf's back also stands on end to make it look bigger to an attacker.

← Wolf

Growlers!

A wolf's growl is a very low, deep sound. They growl to threaten other wolves and to show they have power over a group of wolves, which is called a pack.

Which shark gives a warning before it bites?

The grey reef shark does. If it feels threatened it drops its fins down and raises its snout so that its body is in an 'S' shape. Then it weaves and rolls through the water. If its warning is not taken, the shark will bite before swimming away.

Which big cats hunt in teams?

Unlike most big cats, lions hunt as a team. Female lions, called lionesses, hunt for food while the males and cubs wait for their meal. A group of lionesses can catch larger animals, including zebra, gazelle and wildebeest.

Lionesses hunting

Brown bear

Think

Bears can be scary! Try to think of any friendly bears that appear in films and cartoons.

Which turtle has a deadly bite?

The alligator snapping turtle does. It has a 'beak' made of a tough material. It eats fish, which it lures in with its worm-like tongue, as well as crabs, clams and even other turtles!

When are brown bears deadly?

Brown bears can be deadly if they are injured or weak, or if they are surprised by a human. A mother bear will also defend her cubs by attacking. Since 2000, eight people are known to have been killed by brown bears in North America.

That's rubbish!

Grizzlies, or brown bears, of North America often come into contact with people. The bears come into towns to raid the rubbish bins for something tasty.

Which owl hunts other owls?

The eagle owl does. Eagle owls hunt 'on the wing' (while flying) for any kind of bird, including other owls. As well as hunting in the air, these owls hunt on the ground for insects, reptiles and mammals. The eagle owl is the biggest owl.

Eagle owl

Count

An octopus has eight tentacles. How many tentacles would three octopuses have?

22

What do fleas eat?

Fleas live on most furry animals, and sometimes humans. They jump from animal to animal feeding on blood and can spread disease. Fleas were responsible for spreading the 'black death', a disease that killed millions of people in the 14th century.

Blue-ringed octopus

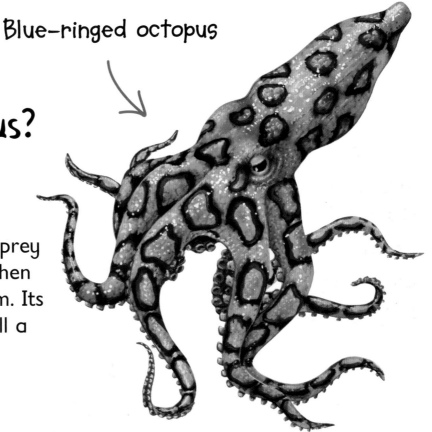

What is the deadliest octopus?

The blue-ringed octopus is the world's most dangerous octopus – and it's only 10 to 20 centimetres long. It grabs prey with its sticky tentacles and then gives a bite that injects venom. Its venom is strong enough to kill a human in four minutes!

Silent hunter!

An owl's feathers have fluffy edges. This softens the sound of their wings flapping so they can swoop down on their prey in silence.

Which fish can make itself spiky?

The spiny puffer fish can make itself into a spiky ball when under attack. The fish gulps in lots of water to make its body swell up and its spikes stand on end. This makes predators think twice about attacking the spiky fish.

Spiny puffer fish

Think

Can you puff like a puffer fish? Take a deep breath in. What happens to your body?

When are elephants deadly?

During the breeding season, male elephants, called bulls, become aggressive and fight each other to win a female. One elephant is strong enough to flip over a car.

Web-tastic!

There are about 20,000 types of spider that spin webs to catch their prey. Most of these make a new web every night, after they've eaten the old one!

How do funnel web spiders kill?

Funnel web spiders are very poisonous and have large fangs that are strong enough to bite through your fingernail. Funnel webs bite their prey many times, injecting poison until their victim is dead. These spiders normally eat insects and small lizards.

Funnel web spider

Are polar bears friendly?

Big, fluffy polar bears look friendly, but they are deadly killers. Polar bears are meat eaters. They often wait by holes in the ice for a seal to come up for air. The bear's powerful bite and huge paws means it can kill its prey quickly.

Polar bear

Which reptile squirts poison?

If attacked, the fire salamander squirts out a poison that is harmful to other animals. Fire salamanders look like a cross between a lizard and a frog, and they have colourful patterns on their skin to warn predators that they are poisonous.

↑ Fire salamander

Colour

Draw an outline of a fire salamander and colour it in using five colours.

Burning hot!

The word 'salamander' means 'within fire' in Persian because a long time ago people thought that salamanders could walk through fire. However, this isn't true.

Why do rhinos charge?

Female rhinos protect their calves by charging at enemies. Rhinos have bad eyesight, but excellent senses of smell and hearing. They can quickly sense if there is a threat nearby. A charging rhino can reach a speed of 50 kilometres an hour!

Which deadly creature lives in a shell?

The cone shell is a type of snail that lives in the sea. Instead of chasing its prey, it sits and waits for creatures to come close. It has a long, tongue-like arm that it uses to shoot a poisonous dart into its victim.

Cone shell

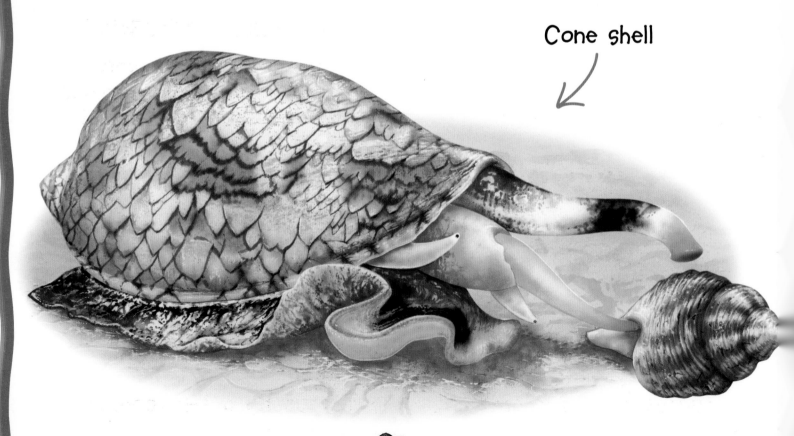

Make

Using a cardboard box, make your own shell. Paint a pattern on it like the cone shell's.

Do killer bees really exist?

Yes, they do! A scientist tried to create bees that made more honey than normal, but instead he created 'killer bees'. They attack in large groups and around 1000 people have been killed by these minibeasts.

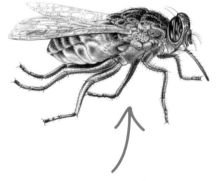

Droppings delight!

Lots of insects find animal droppings delicious. Some beetles lay their eggs in steaming piles of droppings, so that when the eggs hatch the young insects can eat the dung!

How do flies spread diseases?

Tsetse flies spread disease when they feed. They bite and suck blood from one animal and then another, leaving germs behind. These germs can cause 'sleeping sickness' in humans, which makes you want to sleep all the time.

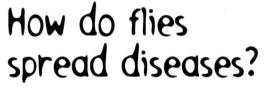

Tsetse fly before feeding   Tsetse fly after feeding

Quiz time

Do you remember what you have read about deadly creatures? These questions will test your memory. The pictures will help you. If you get stuck, read the pages again.

page 8

3. Which deadly fish looks like a stone?

page 11

4. Do snakes eat people?

page 5

1. Which bird can kill while it flies?

page 12

5. What is a black widow?

2. Which creature kills with its tail?

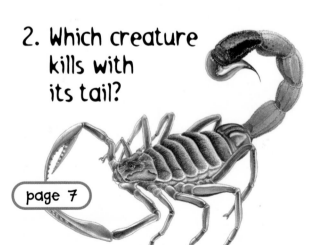

page 7

6. When is jelly dangerous?

page 15

7. What is the deadliest lizard?

page 16

11. What is the deadliest octopus?

page 23

8. Which shark gives a warning before it bites?

page 19

12. Which fish can make itself spiky?

page 24

page 29

13. Do killer bees really exist?

page 20

9. Which big cats hunt in teams?

10. Which turtle has a deadly bite?

page 21

Answers

1. The peregrine falcon
2. Scorpions do
3. The stonefish
4. Some types of python have but this is very rare
5. One of the world's deadliest spiders
6. When it's an Australian box jellyfish
7. The Komodo dragon
8. The grey reef shark
9. Lions do
10. The alligator snapping turtle
11. The blue-ringed octopus
12. The spiny puffer fish
13. Yes, they do

Index